Teens
and
ADDICTION

By Sherri Mabry Gordon

ReferencePoint
Press®

San Diego, CA

TEEN
Health
and
Safety

Content Consultant: Matthew J. Corrigan, Associate Professor and MSW Program Director, Department of Sociology, Anthropology, and Social Work, Seton Hall University

LIBRARY OF CONGRESS CATALOGING-IN-PUBLICATION DATA

Name: Gordon, Sherri Mabry, author.
Title: Teens and Addiction / by Sherri Mabry Gordon
Description: San Diego, CA : ReferencePoint Press, Inc., [2019] | Series:
    Teen Health and Safety | Audience: Grade 9 to 12. | Includes
    bibliographical references and index.
Identifiers: LCCN 2018011548 (print) | LCCN 2018012031 (ebook) | ISBN
    9781682825044 (ebook) | ISBN 9781682825037 (hardback)
Subjects: LCSH: Teenagers—Substance use—Juvenile literature. |
    Teenagers—Drug use—Juvenile literature. | Teenagers—Alcohol
    use—Juvenile literature. | Addicts—Juvenile literature. | Compulsive
    behavior—Juvenile literature.
Classification: LCC HV4999.Y68 (ebook) | LCC HV4999.Y68 G67 2019 (print) |
    DDC 362.290835—dc23
LC record available at https://lccn.loc.gov/2018011548

CONTENTS

Introduction

WHAT DOES ADDICTION LOOK LIKE?

Tracey Helton Mitchell's descent into addiction began as a teenager. Her addiction began when she was given prescription opioids after having her wisdom teeth removed. Although the pills were prescribed for pain, she became addicted to how the pills made her feel. She liked the fact that she could escape her problems and numb any emotional pain she was feeling. As a result, she began abusing prescription opioid painkillers.

> **"When I took opiates, all my problems seemed to melt away. All my troubles disappeared in that moment. I went on chasing that feeling for ten more years, eight of which were in active addiction."[1]**
>
> —Tracey Helton Mitchell, formerly addicted to opioids

"I never realized something as small as a pill could have such huge effects on my life," she says. "Opiates were the solutions I had been looking for, all in one place. When I took opiates, all my problems seemed to melt away. All my troubles disappeared in that moment. I went on chasing that feeling for ten more years, eight of which were in active addiction."[1]

Men are more likely than women to have an alcohol use disorder. Alcohol use disorder is commonly referred to as alcoholism.

Even though Mitchell was a good student with a bright future ahead of her, she was never satisfied with her life. This feeling of dissatisfaction with life is very common among addicted people, she notes. Like her, people who are addicted are often looking to dull the pain they feel from loneliness, depression, anxiety, fear, and more.

Addiction is just as much about being emotionally dependent on a substance as it is about being chemically dependent. People who are chemically dependent are addicted to the chemical properties in a particular substance. This dependence on drugs and alcohol becomes a way of coping with the things in life that seem too big to handle. What's more, addiction gives people a false sense of hope. When the high wears off the problems are still there. And the price people struggling with addiction pay is often steep.

For example, years of drug use took a toll on Mitchell. In the end, she was homeless and did not have any friends left. She also had multiple infections from using unsterile needles and had become extremely thin. She was even arrested. In fact, being arrested was the wake-up call that Mitchell needed to change her life.

"I was finally able to stop using drugs, but not before I had spiraled into a place I never imagined possible for a person like me," she says. "While many users never get to the places I went, the feelings are the same. There is that overwhelming feeling that there is no escape. The task of quitting seems insurmountable. The pain of daily use slowly wrings the joy out of life, to a point where an all-consuming, painful habit dictates your thoughts and feelings."[2]

> **"Drug addiction is a complex disease, and quitting usually takes more than good intentions or a strong will. Drugs change the brain in ways that make quitting hard, even for those that want to."[3]**
>
> —National Institute on Drug Abuse

The National Institute on Drug Abuse (NIDA) notes that it's difficult for people to overcome addiction: "Drug addiction is a complex disease, and quitting usually takes more than good intentions or a strong will. Drugs change the brain in ways that make quitting hard, even for those that want to." However, NIDA recognizes that there is hope for people who want to recover from addiction, "Fortunately, researchers know more than ever about how drugs affect the brain and have found treatments that can help people recover from drug addiction and lead productive lives."[3]

According to Mitchell, there are many paths to recovery. For her, ending addiction included participating in a twelve-step program and going to a rehabilitation facility. Some people in her position also need opioid replacement therapy, as well as counseling. What's more, Mitchell says the process of discontinuing drugs is not easy and can be painful. But after the initial discomfort, she started to feel better. "The important thing to remember is that you can get your life back," she says. "Within less than a week, your whole life *can* start to turn for the better. I am living proof that recovery is possible."[4]

Addiction is a complex problem that can affect anyone regardless of age, race, or socioeconomic background. No one knows for sure why one person develops an addiction while another does not. But there are a number of risk factors involved—including everything from genetics to the age at which a person starts using.

Drug abuse can have a harsh impact on the body. People with long-term addictions can develop lung and heart disease, mental disorders, and cancer. In addition, thousands of people die every year from drug overdoses. Drug abuse also has negative effects on mental functions and can hurt people's memory and ability to learn.

However, addictions can be successfully treated. People with addictions can receive medical care to help wean them off drugs, and they can join treatment programs and support groups. NIDA notes that drug treatment programs teach people with addictions how to stop compulsively seeking and using drugs. "Treatment can occur in a variety of settings, take many different forms, and last for different lengths of time," says NIDA. "The specific type of treatment or combination of treatments will vary depending on the patient's individual needs and, often, on the types of drugs they use."[5]

Chapter 1

WHAT IS ADDICTION?

For years most people assumed individuals with addictions were weak, immoral, and selfish. They believed that if someone truly wanted to quit using a drug then he could simply stop. But researchers now know that quitting a substance is not quite that simple.

In 2011, the American Society of Addiction Medicine—a medical society that focuses on addiction treatment—redefined addiction. It is no longer viewed as a choice. Now the medical community, including the American Medical Association, views addiction as a chronic brain disease. This is because addiction impacts the brain's wiring and alters it permanently. As a result, when someone is addicted, he compulsively pursues the source of his addiction despite the fact that it harms his health, schoolwork, friendships, and more. Even if he feels like stopping, he cannot do so without help. Over time, if the addiction is not treated, it becomes more severe. And it can even become disabling and life-threatening.

To make sense of addiction as a disease, it helps to think of it in much the same way people view diabetes. Just as people with diabetes have to manage their condition for the rest of their lives by eating right, exercising, and adjusting their insulin intake, people with addictions also must manage their disease for the rest of their lives.

Teens can participate in treatment programs. This can help them recover from addiction.

What's more, people struggling with addiction are not cured just because they stop using. For an individual to maintain her sobriety, she needs a solid treatment plan and a good support network. She also has to manage her condition for the rest of her life.

Why Addiction Is a Disease

Some people feel that addiction should not be considered a disease. They believe calling it a disease lets people suffering from addictions off the hook for poor choices and bad behavior. But what researchers have found is that while a person makes the initial choice to try a drug or to drink alcohol, once the brain has been changed by the substance she can lose control over her behavior. And she cannot just stop using—she needs some type of help or intervention. People with addictions usually need intensive treatment and a lifelong treatment plan to manage the disease.

What's more, the choice to try a drug or alcohol does not determine whether or not a person will get addicted. People frequently make unhealthy choices. Sometimes they are faced with disease as a result of those choices and sometimes not. For example, choosing to use tanning beds or spend long hours in the sun without sunscreen could cause a person to get skin cancer. Or that person may never have to deal with the disease. The same is true with addiction. Just like using a tanning bed may or may not cause skin cancer, drinking alcohol may or may not cause an addiction.

The Connection Between Addiction and Mental Illness

Demi Lovato is a singer and songwriter. In her YouTube documentary, *Demi Lovato: Simply Complicated*, Lovato talks in detail about her mental health issues and drug addiction. Like some young people who struggle with addiction, Lovato was also battling mental health issues in addition to her addiction. She was struggling with bipolar disorder, self-harm, and bulimia. Together, these mental health issues increased the risk factors that Lovato would also become addicted to drugs. And because she started using at a young age, before her brain had fully developed, the stage was set for addiction.

"Growing up, I had been bullied in school. And I felt like an outsider; I felt like an outcast," Lovato says. "At that time, I became friends with a girl who was popular. And, one day, I asked her, 'How do you have all these friends?' And she was like, 'Well, do you party?' I was like, 'What do you mean?' And she asked me, 'Do you drink?' We experienced a lot of stuff together, drinking, and using."[6]

Like many teens, Lovato used alcohol and drugs as a way to make friends. But her mental health issues also contributed to her growing addiction. With bipolar disorder, people like Lovato experience periods of intense depression alternating with episodes of high energy or mania. "When I got diagnosed with bipolar disorder, it just made sense," Lovato says. "When I was younger, I didn't know why I would stay up so late writing and playing music. And then I learned about episodes of mania. And I realized that that's probably what it was; I was manic. In a way, I knew that it wasn't my fault anymore. Something was actually off with me."[7]

According to the Substance Abuse and Mental Health Services Administration (SAMHSA), people with bipolar disorder might use drugs to self-medicate. SAMHSA also notes that people with bipolar disorder have more substance abuse issues than people with other mental illnesses.

> "When I got diagnosed with bipolar disorder, it just made sense. . . . In a way, I knew that it wasn't my fault anymore. Something was actually off with me."[7]
>
> —Demi Lovato, singer

Lovato was also struggling with an eating disorder known as bulimia. Lovato struggled with body image issues and trying to lose weight. She didn't like the way she looked and wanted to be thinner. As a result, she addressed her body image issues in an unhealthy way. Eventually, her unhealthy habits became a full-fledged eating disorder.

The National Institute of Mental Health states that approximately 3 percent of teenagers are impacted by an eating disorder. Eating disorders also increase a person's risk of substance abuse. In fact, teens with eating disorders are five times likelier to abuse substances than the general population. However, substance abuse is not the same thing as addiction. People who abuse substances often use too much of the substance, but they are able to quit and recover with little or no treatment.

"My first time doing coke, I was 17, working on Disney Channel and I was with a couple of friends," Lovato recounts. "I was scared because my mom always told me that your heart could just burst if you do it. But I did it anyways, and I loved it. I felt out of control with coke the first time that I did it. My dad was an addict and an alcoholic. And, I guess I always searched for what he found in drugs and alcohol because it fulfilled him and he chose that over a family."[8]

> "My dad was an addict and an alcoholic. And, I guess I always searched for what he found in drugs and alcohol because it fulfilled him and he chose that over a family."[8]
>
> —Demi Lovato, singer

From there, Lovato's substance abuse started to grow into an addiction. During the peak of her addiction, she was snorting cocaine every 30 to 60 minutes and drinking a soda bottle filled with vodka every morning. By the time she was eighteen, her addiction had spiraled out of control and she had a breakdown during a tour. At one point, she even hit a back-up dancer for telling others that Lovato was abusing Adderall, a prescription drug used to treat attention deficit hyperactivity disorder. It was then that Lovato's family and management team intervened and she quit the tour to get treatment.

Not long after Lovato completed her treatment program, she started using drugs and alcohol again. Once out of the program, Lovato says, "I wasn't ready to get sober. I was sneaking it on planes, sneaking it in bathrooms, sneaking it throughout the night. Nobody knew."[9]

One night, she did cocaine and took Xanax, which is a prescription drug normally used to treat anxiety. "I started to choke a little bit," she recalls. "My heart started racing, and I remember thinking, 'Oh my God, I might be overdosing right now.'"[10]

Overdosing occurs when a person takes more of a substance than their body can handle. In an actual overdose, the person may have difficulty breathing and lose consciousness. In this situation, Lovato did not overdose, and the fear she had felt did not deter her from using again. She continued to use drugs and alcohol and became very difficult to be around. "I was not easy to work with," Lovato admits. "I didn't feel anything. I didn't feel guilty. I didn't feel embarrassed. I would sneak out,

In 2018, Demi Lovato was sober. She was also recovering from her eating disorder.

get drugs. I would fake my drug tests with other people's pee, and I'd lie straight to their faces. It's embarrassing to look back at the person that I was."[11]

Things finally hit rock bottom when everyone on Lovato's management team told her that there was nothing more they could do for her. At one point, she started crying and asking what she needed to do. Members of her management team told her to give them her cell phone. "This [phone] was the gateway to everything," Phil McIntyre, Lovato's manager, recalls telling her. "This was the wrong people, it was drug dealers, it was a lot of the negative influences in her life were coming through the cell phone."[12] Lovato smashed her phone and dunked it into water.

That push from her management team was what she needed. From there, the entire trajectory of her life changed. Lovato began to seriously address her addiction and mental health issues. She even lived in a sober-living facility for almost one year just so she could stay clean. In March 2017, Lovato celebrated five years of sobriety. She is an activist for mental health bullying prevention and continues to encourage others through her music.

A Closer Look at Comorbidity

Like Lovato, some people who battle addiction are also diagnosed with mental disorders. When a person has both an addiction and a mental disorder this is called comorbidity or co-occurrence. Research shows that people diagnosed with mood or anxiety disorders are twice as likely to struggle with substance abuse or addiction. The same is true for people with an antisocial personality or a conduct disorder.

Even though mental illness and addiction can occur at the same time, it does not necessarily mean that one causes the other. For example, Lovato's addiction did not cause her bipolar disorder. Instead, drugs and alcohol are often used by people with mental health issues to escape and to self-medicate. This is especially true for people with depression and anxiety.

Drugs and alcohol can make the symptoms of a mental health problem worse. They may also trigger new symptoms. What's more, drugs and alcohol interact with medications such as antidepressants and antianxiety pills and make them less effective. To make matters worse, it is difficult to diagnose an addiction and a co-occurring mental health issue. It takes a lot of time to determine what symptoms are related to addiction and what might be a mental disorder. What's more, if a patient is in denial about either issue, this can make diagnosis even more challenging.

Depression can take a significant toll on people's mental health. Sometimes people with depression abuse drugs to self-medicate.

Types of Addiction

According to the Center on Addiction, a nonprofit group that wants to end addiction in the United States, it is common for people to have multiple addictions. More than one-half of people with a substance abuse problem also have issues with other substances. For instance, nearly three-fourths of people with a prescription drug addiction also have another substance problem. Meanwhile, two-thirds of those addicted to illegal drugs struggle with another substance problem. And one-third of people with alcohol use disorders have a problem with nicotine or other drugs.

When most people think of addiction, they tend to think of drug addiction and alcohol use disorder. But addiction can cover more than just drugs and alcohol. There are both substance addictions and behavioral addictions. Some common substance addictions include alcohol; illegal drugs such as heroin, cocaine, and meth; prescription drugs such as painkillers, sleeping pills, and antianxiety medications; and nicotine products such as cigarettes, e-cigarettes, and tobacco. Meanwhile, some common behavioral addictions include gambling, pornography, video games, social media, and using the internet.

According to a 2012 study in the *International Journal of Preventative Medicine*, an "Internet addiction is similar to a drug addiction except that in the former, the individual is not addicted to a substance but the behavior. . . . In addition, the physical signs of drug addiction are absent in behavioral addiction."[13] The study goes on to note that people with behavioral addictions suffer similar consequences as people who abuse drugs and alcohol.

People with substance abuse problems may also struggle with behavioral addictions. When this occurs it is called co-addiction. Some research suggests that people with behavioral addictions experience similar changes in the brain as those with addiction to substances. They also may have common risk factors, including everything from genetics to exposure at a young age. Also, people struggling with behavioral addictions may exhibit the same behaviors as those with substance abuse addictions, such as changes in his or her behavior, appearance, and moods. These findings suggest that addiction is a disease that can be expressed in multiple ways.

"Yet, unfortunately, too often, [addiction is] not talked about openly and honestly. It's whispered about. It's met with derision and scorn."[14]

—Michael Botticelli, President Barack Obama's Director of Drug Policy

Millions of People Are Impacted by Addiction

Nationwide, many people are affected by addiction in

some way. Addiction can occur in a person's family, in his school, or in his neighborhood. Addiction is not a small issue. More than 23 million people over the age of twelve are addicted to a substance, according to the National Council on Alcoholism and Drug Dependence (NCADD). When it comes to teens, alcohol is the most widely abused substance. A large number of people begin drinking when they are very young.

In one study by the Center on Addiction at Columbia University, 90 percent of people with an addiction began using alcohol or other drugs before turning eighteen. Learning more about the consequences of addiction can help teens before it becomes an issue in their lives. "Yet, unfortunately, too often, [addiction is] not talked about openly and honestly. It's whispered about. It's met with derision and scorn," says Michael Botticelli, who was President Barack Obama's Director of Drug Policy.[14]

JUST HOW BIG IS THE PROBLEM?

Addiction is an issue that impacts millions of people every day. According to Addiction Center, an organization that works with treatment centers to help addicted people, 2.6 million Americans over the age of twelve have a dependence on both alcohol and illicit drugs.

Addiction is an issue among teens and young adults. According to NCADD, approximately four out of five college students drink alcohol and about one-half of them engage in binge drinking. Binge drinking occurs when a person drinks large quantities of alcohol in a short amount of time. The impacts of this drinking are significant. For example, 5,000 people under the age of twenty-one die each year in alcohol-related deaths, and more than 97,000 students between the ages of eighteen and twenty-four are victims of alcohol-related date rape or sexual assault.

Why Teens Start Using

It is not uncommon for young people to be rebellious, impulsive, and curious during their teen years. But these tendencies also can lead to addiction—especially if they are combined with drugs and alcohol. A survey sponsored by NIDA showed that the number of teens using or trying drugs in 2017 increased compared to previous years. The risk of addiction is an issue for young adults. When it comes to addiction, more than one-half of new drug users are under the age of eighteen. The majority of adults with an addiction first experimented with drugs before they turned twenty-one.

Partnership for Drug-Free Kids, a nonprofit organization focused on helping families who have addicted children, notes that some of the most common reasons that teens try drugs or alcohol include curiosity, peer pressure, stress, family environment, emotional struggles, and a desire to escape reality. Many teens who start abusing drugs or alcohol are following along with their friends. To many teens, drinking or using drugs may seem like part of the normal teen experience—especially if their friends are drinking, smoking pot, using e-cigarettes, and doing other drugs. Sometimes their friends will urge them to try a substance and sometimes teens try it simply because it is readily available. Teens are also influenced by what they see their parents and other adults doing. If their parents regularly use alcohol, drugs, or cigarettes to cope with emotions such as stress, then teens see that behavior as a normal coping mechanism.

Partnership for Drug-Free Kids also states that the media can make teens susceptible to drug and alcohol use. Music, movies, and advertisements frequently glamorize drinking, smoking, and drug use. In fact, 45 percent of teens agree with the statement: "The music that teens listen to makes marijuana seem cool." In addition, 45 percent of teens also agree with this statement: "Movies and TV shows make drugs seem like an OK thing to do."[15]

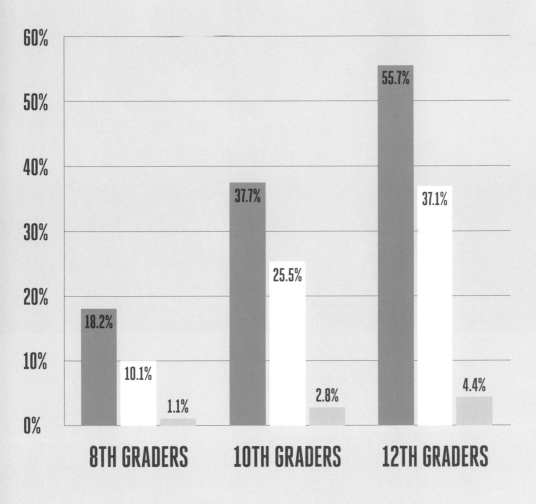

ALCOHOL ●   MARIJUANA ○   HALLUCINOGENS ●

8TH GRADERS
- 18.2%
- 10.1%
- 1.1%

10TH GRADERS
- 37.7%
- 25.5%
- 2.8%

12TH GRADERS
- 55.7%
- 37.1%
- 4.4%

TEEN DRUG USE IN 2017

In 2017, NIDA presented survey findings that showed teen drug use within the previous year. NIDA found that older teens use substances more frequently than younger teens.

Teens with social anxiety can struggle in certain social situations. Because of this, they might avoid social interactions and activities.

Some teens turn to drugs and alcohol to escape reality or to self-medicate. When teens are unhappy, lonely, anxious, depressed, or struggling with other life issues, they may use substances to escape or to numb their pain. Depending on what substance they try, they may feel a lot like Tracey Helton Mitchell did—that their troubles just melted away. "When teens are unhappy and can't find a healthy outlet for their frustration or a trusted confidant, they may turn to chemicals for solace," said the experts at the Partnership for Drug-Free Kids. "Depending on what substance they're trying, they may feel blissfully oblivious, wonderfully happy or energized and confident."[16]

Meanwhile, other teens will turn to drugs to improve their energy and academic focus. This is especially true if they are perfectionists and feel the pressure to perform well on tests. Sometimes, teens struggle with boredom and crave excitement in their lives. They also may believe that they need to be doing something all the time. As a result, drugs and alcohol are a way for them to fill the void and emptiness they might feel. Substance use may also seem like an exciting and fun way to bond with other teens.

Experts note that many times teens want to assert their independence, so they rebel against authority. As a result, some teens look to drugs, alcohol, and cigarettes as the vehicle for flaunting their freedom. Some teens may also look to drugs and alcohol as a way to release anger. Meanwhile other teens might turn to substances, especially cigarettes, to make their parents or other adults in their lives angry.

For shy or introverted teenagers, social situations can be particularly challenging. As a result, these teens might try alcohol or drugs as a way of boosting their confidence, lowering their inhibitions, and dealing with social anxiety. What's more, many teens believe that if they do or say something stupid, no one will hold it against them because they were under the influence.

Unfortunately, many teens do not realize the risks that substance abuse and addiction pose. For instance, many teens believe that e-cigarettes are a healthy alternative to smoking and do not realize that inhaling any foreign substance into your lungs is not healthy. Additionally, teens are often willing to believe a friend who assures them that the risks of using a drug or alcohol are minimal. For this reason, it is important that teens know the facts about addiction.

Chapter 2

WHAT CAUSES ADDICTION?

Addiction runs in Matt's family. His father is recovering from alcohol use disorder and his mother has been trying to quit smoking for years. Meanwhile, his cousin has been in and out of treatment for heroin, and now his younger brother is addicted to meth. "Heart disease runs in some families," Matt says. "Addiction runs in ours. . . . I look at addiction as our own family monster, chasing us through the generations."[17]

> "Heart disease runs in some families. Addiction runs in ours. . . . I look at addiction as our own family monster, chasing us through the generations."[17]
>
> —Matt, an individual who has seen addiction in his family

Matt's younger brother, Stephen, was a junior in high school when the family noticed changes in his behavior. He started picking fights and was very jumpy. At first, they assumed this was normal teenage behavior. But then they found out he had been smoking meth. When their mother kicked Stephen out of the house, he went to live with Matt. But things were still rocky. Stephen wasn't himself, and it was frustrating for Matt. Then one day, Matt found Stephen smoking meth in his house. He told him to either get into a treatment program or move out. Stephen decided to move out. "He got in my face and told me to leave him alone," Matt says. "He was sick of everybody always trying to control him. . . . He stays somewhere else now, but I call him to see how he's doing."[18]

Matt says his brother is not ready to quit, but Matt wants to be ready to help Stephen when he decides to. Matt called a drug abuse hotline to ask for help. One of the best ways to help an addicted person is to learn everything you can about addiction. "I know I can't make my brother quit using meth, and it makes me sad," Matt says. "But at least I am learning about meth addiction and things that can help when he's finally ready to quit."[19]

Drug use is not uncommon. According to NIDA, by the time teens are seniors in high school, more than one-half of them have tried alcohol. Meanwhile, one-half of them will have taken an illegal drug and nearly 40 percent will have smoked a cigarette. In addition, more than 20 percent of seniors in high school will have used a prescription drug without a prescription.

Substance Abuse and the Teen Brain

The part of the brain that's responsible for making decisions and choices is not fully developed until a person is in their mid-twenties. This is one of the reasons why young people often take more risks than people who are older. NIDA explains, "Adolescents are 'biologically wired' to seek new experiences and take risks, as well as to carve out their own identity. Trying drugs may fulfill all these normal developmental drives, but in an unhealthy way that can have very serious long-term consequences."[20]

Additionally, because the teen brain is still developing and changing, teens who use drugs or drink alcohol are at a greater risk

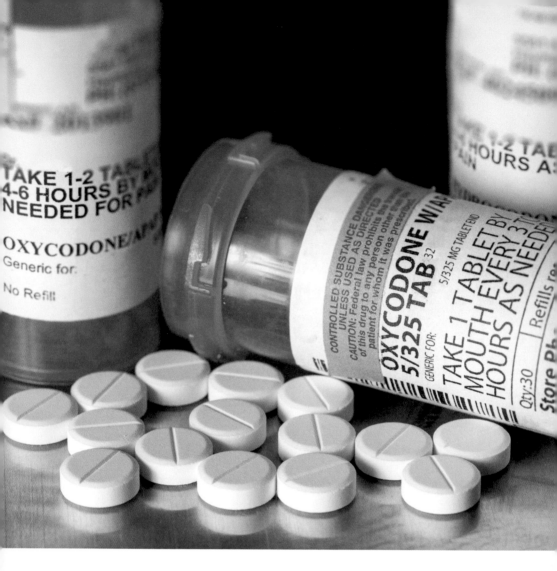

Oxycodone is an opioid pain reliever. It is one example of a prescription drug that's often misused.

of damaging their brains long-term. Aside from forming an addiction, teens who abuse substances may lose their ability to control their impulses. Even a person's attention span and learning abilities can be impacted by substance abuse.

To better understand how this can happen, it helps to know what drugs and alcohol do to a person's brain. One of the biggest ways they affect the brain is changing the way synapses are formed.

Synapses occur where nerve cells connect with other nerve cells. For example, each time a new skill is learned or a new memory is formed, stronger connections, or synapses, are created between brain cells. The structure of the brain's connections is formed based on that experience.

Because the teen brain builds connections faster than an adult's, teens can become addicted much more quickly than adults. Using alcohol and drugs before the brain has fully developed increases a person's risk for future addiction dramatically. For instance, teens who start drinking alcohol before age fifteen are five times more likely to develop an addiction to alcohol than those who first use alcohol when they are twenty-one or older.

How an Addiction Is Developed

People feel pleasure when their basic needs are met, such as eating a meal or drinking a cold glass of water on a hot day. In most cases, these feel-good feelings are caused by the release of certain chemicals in the brain, such as dopamine.

Dopamine is the chemical messenger that creates pleasure in the body. Sometimes when teens abuse substances, those substances take control of the reward pathway and cause large amounts of dopamine to flood the brain. The reward pathway tells people to repeat actions that are pleasurable. Because of this, it is easy for drugs and alcohol to hijack the reward pathway and teach people to use harmful substances continually.

Once a person has used drugs or alcohol for a while, the brain adjusts to these increases in dopamine. The brain may begin to reduce the number of dopamine receptors or make less dopamine. "The brain adapts to the dopamine surges by producing less

UNDERSTANDING THE REWARD PATHWAY

The reward pathway plays an important role in how drugs impact the brain. The reward pathway involves several parts of the brain, including the prefrontal cortex, the ventral tegmental area (VTA), and the nucleus accumbens. When a person does something rewarding, this information travels to the VTA, then the nucleus accumbens, and then to the prefrontal cortex. When this pathway is used, it teaches the person to repeat a pleasurable activity again and again.

One way that this rewarding information is communicated to the brain is through the release of dopamine. When some drugs are taken, they can cause the brain to release up to ten times the amount of dopamine that is released when doing something naturally rewarding, such as exercising. What's more, the pleasurable effects can last much longer than those produced by natural rewards. As a result, this reward is so powerful that it impacts the brain and prompts people to continually use drugs.

dopamine," notes NCADD. "The user must therefore keep abusing drugs to bring his or her dopamine function back to 'normal.'"[21]

With less dopamine signaling the brain, a person's ability to feel pleasure is reduced. She may no longer get much pleasure from using the same amount of drugs or alcohol. This is known as tolerance. In an attempt to bring dopamine levels back up, the person may start taking in more of the substance.

Another area of the teen brain that is impacted by addiction is the prefrontal cortex. This part of the brain helps with decision-making. Since this part of the brain is not fully developed in teens, it can become damaged through substance abuse. "The adolescent brain is often likened to a car with a fully functioning gas pedal (the reward system) but weak brakes (the prefrontal cortex)," explain experts at NIDA. "Teenagers are highly motivated to pursue pleasurable rewards

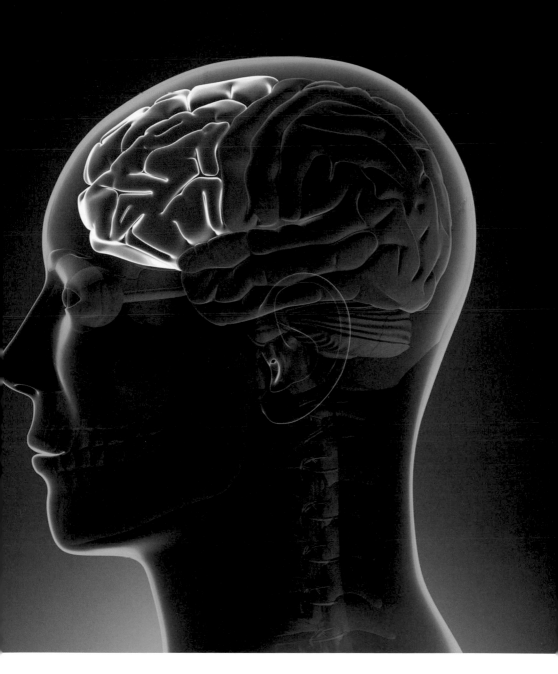

The prefrontal cortex is in the brain's frontal lobe. This area plays a role in the reward pathway.

and avoid pain, but their judgment and decision-making skills are still limited. This affects their ability to weigh risks accurately and make sound decisions, including decisions about using drugs."[22]

Experts at NIDA also note, "Chronic drug use not only realigns a person's priorities but also may alter key brain areas necessary for judgment and self-control. . . . This is why, despite popular belief, willpower alone is often insufficient to overcome an addiction. Drug use has compromised the very parts of the brain that make it possible to 'say no.'"[23]

To overcome an addiction, Dr. Michael Bierer, an assistant professor at Harvard Medical School, says people who abuse drugs need to find new ways to feel pleasure. He notes that social and physical activities are healthy ways to do this.

There is no one factor that can predict whether or not a person will develop an addiction, according to NCADD. The risk for addiction is influenced by a combination of factors. These factors include biology, social environment, and the age of the person abusing the substance. The more risk factors an individual has, the greater his chance of addiction.

Genes and Addiction

Each person's genes contain information that determine their traits. For instance, genes determine factors including what color a person's hair will be or how tall she will be. Experts at NCADD note that biology plays a large role in addiction: "The genes that people are born with—in combination with environmental influences—account for about half of their addiction vulnerability. Additionally, gender, ethnicity,

> "The genes that people are born with—in combination with environmental influences—account for about half of their addiction vulnerability."[24]
>
> —National Council on Alcoholism and Drug Dependence

Twin studies are helpful to many types of research. The studies can help show how much a person is shaped by their genetics and their environment.

and the presence of other mental disorders may influence the risk for drug abuse and addiction."[24]

One of the most common risk factors for addiction includes having an immediate family member with an addiction. While any relative with a history of addiction increases a person's risk, a relative such as a parent or a sibling makes addiction even more likely to occur. If a teen has a family history of addiction, he or she is four times more likely to develop a problem, according to NCADD. As a result, addiction often runs in families.

Studies on identical and fraternal twins help researchers understand how genetics play a role in addiction. Identical twins are very similar genetically—they are the same sex and usually have similar physical characteristics. But fraternal twins share about one-half of their genetic makeup with each other. In one study of identical and fraternal twins, researchers discovered that when one identical twin was addicted to alcohol, the other twin had a high chance of being addicted as well. But when one fraternal twin was addicted to alcohol, the other twin did not necessarily have an addiction. Based on the differences between the identical and fraternal twins, the study found that 50 to 60 percent of addiction is due to genetic factors.

Researchers are looking for specific biological differences that might make people more or less vulnerable to addiction. For instance, it may be harder for people with certain genes to quit abusing a substance once they start. Likewise, there also might be genetic factors that make it harder for people to become addicted. As a result, researchers often study large families to see which genes might make them susceptible to addiction. One way they do that is by comparing DNA sequences of family members struggling with addiction with those who are not. Researchers look for pieces of DNA that are shared among family members with addiction and are less common in those who are not addicted. DNA is a long molecule found within most of the body's cells. It contains genetic information.

Aside from determining if a person inherited a tendency to addiction or not, another goal of genetic research is to improve treatments for addiction. With each addiction gene that scientists identify comes a potential target for improved treatment. Researchers can focus on that gene and develop a drug that modifies its activity. Researchers hope that in doing so, the signals or pathways in the brain that are impacted by addiction can be changed and corrected. And, in the future, scientists hope to develop genetic tests that allow them to determine which medications would be most effective in treating addiction. The goal is to be able to tailor treatment programs for each individual based on his or her genetic makeup.

Withdrawal symptoms are another factor influenced by genetics. Withdrawal occurs when a person is chemically dependent on a drug and stops taking the drug. Withdrawal symptoms can include shaking, vomiting, and anxiety. People may experience withdrawal symptoms in varying degrees depending on their genetics. Withdrawal can be a very dangerous process and should not be attempted without professional help. Depending on what the person is addicted to, he runs the risk of seizures, hallucinations, rapid heart rate, and even death. "Detoxification, the process by which the body clears itself of drugs . . . is often accompanied by unpleasant and potentially fatal side effects stemming from withdrawal," notes NIDA. "Detoxification is often managed with medications administered by a physician."[25]

> "Detoxification, the process by which the body clears itself of drugs . . . is often accompanied by unpleasant and potentially fatal side effects stemming from withdrawal."[25]
>
> —National Institute on Drug Abuse

Environment and Addiction

In addition to biology, a person's environment also influences the development of addiction. The type of parenting a teen receives can play a role. For instance, parental neglect makes people more prone to addiction. Poor parental supervision can also lead to easy access to drugs and alcohol.

Teens who are dealing with peer pressure or who have a history of sexual abuse, physical abuse, or other traumatic events during childhood also are at an increased risk of developing an addiction. In these cases, people will sometimes deal with their emotions by self-medicating with drugs or alcohol. In these situations, "the

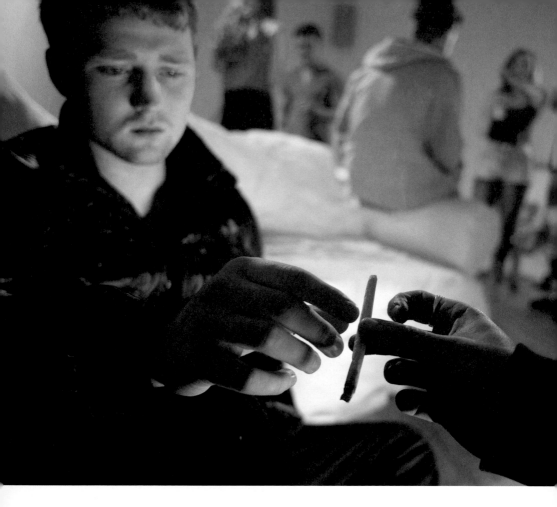

Teens faced with peer pressure can end up trying things they aren't comfortable with. Smoking cigarettes or marijuana is one example of this.

problematic behavior is used not to have a good time, but as an emotional coping mechanism," says addiction expert Robert Weiss. He notes that people struggling with addiction "are not trying to feel good, they're trying to feel less. They want to escape stress, anxiety, depression and other forms of emotional discomfort, and they use their addiction to do that."[26]

There's also a greater risk for addiction when teens come from low-income homes. Even the teen's communication and social skills can play a role in addiction. Many times, kids will use drugs or alcohol to loosen their inhibitions or to give them confidence. They might use substances in order to make friends or to fit in. When this happens, the drugs or alcohol can become a crutch that the teen starts to rely on. She may feel as if she cannot function in social settings without the substance, and eventually she becomes emotionally dependent on the drug. This dependence can lead to addiction.

Even though abusing substances at any age can lead to addiction, the earlier a teen starts drinking or using, the more likely the action will lead to a serious addiction. Because of teens' undeveloped prefrontal cortexes, they are more prone to risk-taking, which might include abusing substances. Every year that substance abuse is delayed, the risk of addiction decreases. The Center on Addiction notes that "people who began using addictive substances before age 15 are nearly 7 times likelier to develop a substance problem that those who delay first use until age 21 or older."[27]

Are Some People Destined to Struggle with Addiction?

Experts caution against assuming just because addiction runs in a family, a person is destined to struggle with addiction. They stress that there are many risk factors associated with addiction, including what type of environment teens grow up in, who they hang out with, and their coping skills. "Just because you are prone to addiction doesn't mean you're going to become addicted," says Dr. Glen Hanson of the University of Utah's Genetic Learning Center. "It just means you've got to be careful."[28]

> "Just because you are prone to addiction doesn't mean you're going to become addicted. It just means you've got to be careful."[28]
>
> —Dr. Glen Hanson of the Genetic Learning Center

Chapter 3

WHAT ARE THE EFFECTS OF ADDICTION?

Will Doerhoff was a model student in high school. He tirelessly volunteered in his community and went to a small Catholic high school in Arkansas. He had never once tried drugs. But when Doerhoff went to college at the University of Arkansas, his life veered off course. After joining a fraternity, Doerhoff started binge drinking and using prescription painkillers. An older member in the fraternity taught Doerhoff how to inject and smoke prescription drugs. By the time Doerhoff returned home from his freshman year of college, he had developed an addiction to heroin.

One day while at home, Doerhoff's mother found him face down and barely alive in his bedroom. He had overdosed on heroin and nearly died. After that, Doerhoff entered a treatment program and was successful in managing his addiction for a little over one year. But when he relapsed, heroin claimed his life. After Doerhoff's death, his parents were surprised to learn about the number of people from his college who knew about his addiction, yet did nothing to intervene. "As parents, had we known early on of this drug abuse, our son would have been home and in treatment as quickly as this began, but the grim reality is that parents and adults are the last to know," his parents said.[29]

After reading the text messages from Doerhoff's fraternity brothers after his death, his parents realized that Doerhoff's peers were either scared or not sure what to do when his drug use began, so they stood by and said nothing. Doerhoff's parents started the William Christian Doerhoff Memorial Foundation to empower teens and young adults to say something when they see the effects of addiction.

> **"As parents, had we known early on of this drug abuse, our son would have been home and in treatment as quickly as this began, but the grim reality is that parents and adults are the last to know."**[29]
>
> —Parents of Will Doerhoff, a college student who died of heroin use

Education and empowerment are keys to saving lives from the effects of addiction. One of the best ways for teens to address the issue is to learn more about how it occurs as well as how it impacts people. If teens understand what is at stake and how harmful substance abuse can be, they may be more likely to speak up the next time they see someone using.

Medical Consequences of Addiction

People who struggle with addiction often have an array of medical issues, including everything from lung and cardiovascular disease to cancer and mental disorders. Imaging scans, chest X-rays, and blood tests often show the extensive damage from long-term addiction on the body. Some addictive drugs even damage or destroy nerve cells in the brain or the nervous system, which impacts everything from cognitive function to memory. In his 2010 journal article in *Addiction Science & Clinical Practice*, Dr. Thomas J. Gould, a professor at Pennsylvania State University, wrote, "The brain regions and processes that underlie addiction overlap extensively with those that are involved in essential cognitive functions, including learning, memory, attention, reasoning, and impulse control."[30]

> "The brain regions and processes that underlie addiction overlap extensively with those that are involved in essential cognitive functions, including learning, memory, attention, reasoning, and impulse control."[30]
>
> —Dr. Thomas J. Gould, professor at Pennsylvania State University

Addiction can also lead to death. Approximately 64,000 Americans died in 2016 from drug overdoses. Many of these deaths were due to opioids, according the Centers for Disease Control and Prevention (CDC). When someone overdoses on opioids, he has taken more of the drug than his body can handle. There are three main symptoms that occur when someone is experiencing an overdose: pinpoint pupils, slowed breathing, and unconsciousness. It is important that the person overdosing receives medical help right away. Slowed breathing is especially dangerous, because it can lead to brain damage and even death due insufficient oxygen getting to the body's organs.

If people's addictions are left untreated, public health experts predict that 650,000 people will die by 2027 from opioids alone. This prediction stems from the opioid epidemic that's sweeping across the United States. "If nothing is done, we can expect a lot of people to die," writes journalist German Lopez about the opioid epidemic.[31]

It's not just opioids that are causing deaths. Tobacco is responsible for almost 6 million deaths each year worldwide and is the leading cause of preventable deaths. Meanwhile, the National Institute on Alcohol Abuse and Alcoholism says approximately 88,000 people

People can overdose the first time they use drugs. Overdoses slow down a person's breathing and can cause death.

die in the United States each year from alcohol-related deaths. This makes alcohol the third-leading cause of preventable death each year.

Addiction can also cause an increase in the spread of diseases. Intravenous injection of drugs, such as heroin, can spread hepatitis C, which is a serious and sometimes fatal liver disease. Additionally, drug and alcohol use can lead to risky sexual behaviors. This can increase the spread of HIV/AIDS, hepatitis B and C, and other sexually transmitted diseases.

Mental Health Consequences of Addiction

In addition to physical issues, addiction also impacts a person's mental health. Drug abuse alters the brain's chemistry. As a result, abusing substances can cause both short- and long-term changes in the brain. These changes can lead to mental health issues such as depression, anxiety, and aggression. People with addictions are twice as likely to suffer from mood and anxiety disorders. One study found that 43.4 million Americans age eighteen and older had some form of mental illness. Of those people, nearly 20 percent had both a mental illness and an addiction. According to NIDA, when it comes to substance abuse disorders and mental health issues, "it's often unclear whether one helped cause the other or if common underlying risk factors contribute to both disorders."[32]

Effects of Specific Substances

The impacts of substance abuse and addiction are significant. Drinking too much alcohol damages the brain and various organs. For instance, alcohol hampers the brain's communication pathways, which can change the way the brain works and the drinker's behavior. One area in the brain that is most vulnerable to alcohol abuse is the cerebral cortex, which is responsible for problem-solving and decision-making. Another area impacted is the hippocampus, which is responsible for memory and learning. The cerebellum, which controls movement and coordination, is also impacted by alcohol. As a result, all of these disruptions in the brain can not only change a person's mood and behavior but also make it harder for someone to think clearly and maintain coordination.

Excessive drinking also impacts the body's other organs, including the heart, liver, and pancreas. For instance, drinking a lot over time, or even just a lot at one time, can cause irregular heartbeats, a stroke, and high blood pressure. Drinking also takes a toll on the liver. One example is cirrhosis of the liver, which is an irreversible disease caused by scar tissue on the liver. Meanwhile, drinking also damages the pancreas, causing it to release toxic substances that can eventually lead to pancreatitis. Pancreatitis is a swelling of the blood vessels that prevents proper digestion. Drinking can even cause different types of cancers, including liver, throat, and breast cancer.

Marijuana is often abused by people in the United States. It harms learning and short-term memory. It also impacts a person's coordination and ability to focus. Using marijuana can also increase a person's heart rate and damage her lungs. It can even trigger psychosis in people that have certain genetic factors. Studies have shown that marijuana has a higher risk of triggering psychosis if the user has a family history of psychotic disorders. In addition, people who have experienced childhood abuse are more likely to experience psychosis when using marijuana. "Those who have psychiatric disorders in their families . . . should bear in mind that they're playing with fire if they smoke pot during adolescence," says Dr. Ran Barzilay, a child and adolescent psychiatrist at Tel Aviv University's Sackler School of Medicine.[33]

> **"Those who have psychiatric disorders in their families . . . should bear in mind that they're playing with fire if they smoke pot during adolescence."[33]**
>
> —Dr. Ran Barzilay, a child and adolescent psychiatrist

Tobacco increases a user's risk of getting heart disease, emphysema, cancer, and bronchial disorders. Bronchial disorders, such as bronchitis, make it hard for people to breathe. According to the CDC, more than 480,000 people die from smoking each year in the United States. The federal agency also notes that smokers tend to die ten years earlier than people who do not smoke. If smoking trends continue, the CDC says, "5.6 million of today's Americans younger than 18 years of age are expected to die prematurely from a smoking-related illness."[34]

"5.6 million of today's Americans younger than 18 years of age are expected to die prematurely from a smoking-related illness."[34]

—Centers for Disease Control and Prevention

Prescription opioid painkillers, such as OxyContin and Vicodin, are misused often. In 2016, 11.5 million Americans misused prescription opioids. This means they did not use the pills in a way that was directed by a doctor. People often crush opioid pain relievers and inject or snort them. Opioids bring the user an intense feeling of euphoria and are therefore quite addictive. Misusing prescription opioids can lead to overdoses. In 2016, approximately 17,000 people died from prescription opioid overdoses, according to the National Center for Health Statistics.

People with addictions to prescription opioids will sometimes switch to heroin. Heroin is an illegal opioid, but it can be easier for people to get than prescription opioids. Heroin impacts the brain the same way that prescription opioids do. It relieves pain and gives the user feelings of euphoria and relaxation. Many people overdose on heroin. The National Center for Health Statistics found that in 2016, more than 15,000 people died from heroin overdoses.

Meth, short for methamphetamine, impacts the central nervous system and is very addictive. Like with opioids, meth gives users an intense sense of euphoria by releasing dopamine in the brain. People who use meth can experience faster breathing, irregular heartbeats, increased blood pressure, a feeling of wakefulness, and less of an appetite than people who don't use meth. In the long term, meth users have dental issues, anxiety, severe itching, and problems sleeping. They also exhibit violent behaviors, paranoia, and hallucinations.

Heroin can be injected intravenously. This causes users to experience a faster high.

MDMA is a drug commonly referred to as Ecstasy or Molly. Users can experience feelings of pleasure, increased energy, and a distortion of their senses and perception of time. MDMA increases dopamine production in the brain. It also increases a user's heart rate and can cause chills, sweating, muscle cramps, nausea, and vision problems. NIDA notes, "High doses of MDMA can affect the body's ability to regulate temperature. This can lead to a spike in body temperature that can occasionally result in liver, kidney, or heart failure or even death."[35]

Some athletes use anabolic steroids to increase athletic performance and muscle mass. But using steroids specifically for performance enhancement is illegal. These drugs are sometimes prescribed to people with anemia, a blood condition, or those who do not produce enough testosterone on their own. People who use anabolic steroids illegally can experience heart disease, stroke, liver issues, acne, and depression.

Addiction and Abuse at Home

Teens who experience physical or sexual abuse are more likely to engage in substance abuse. Two-thirds of the people in treatment for addiction say they experienced physical, sexual, or emotional abuse as a child. Likewise, studies have found that around 80 percent of child abuse cases involve alcohol or drug use. Teens who grow up in homes with an adult who suffers from addiction are more likely to experience some sort of abuse. In addition, according to the American Society of Addiction Medicine, several studies "suggest that substance use/abuse plays a facilitative role in IPV [intimate partner violence] by precipitating or exacerbating violence."[36]

Alcohol and Its Risks for Sexual Abuse

When teens drink alcohol, they put themselves at risk in a number of areas. For example, alcohol could cause teens to have a hangover, perform poorly in school, or miss class. Other times the consequences might be more severe, such as driving under the influence, being hurt or injured, or being taken advantage of sexually.

Teens who drink are more likely to be sexually active. They are also more likely to have unsafe, unprotected sex. In addition, teens who drink are more likely to be involved in fights and commit violent crimes. They are also at a greater risk of using other drugs.

Young adults in college have a greater risk for abuse. According to NCADD, each year "more than 690,000 students between the ages of 18 and 24 are assaulted by another student who has been drinking." NCADD also notes that each year, "more than 97,000 students between the ages of 18 and 24 are victims of alcohol-related sexual assault or date rape."[37] Studies have also shown that alcohol is involved with at least 50 percent of all sexual assaults on college students.

A person can be a victim of sexual assault if she drinks a beverage that has been spiked with a date rape drug. Types of date rape drugs include Rohypnol and ketamine.

There might be unhealthy mindsets at play when sexual assault and alcohol use exist together. For instance, some men believe that women who drink are interested in engaging in sexual activity. As a result of this mindset, some men may feel justified in sexually assaulting women. But being under the influence is never an excuse for violating a person's body.

Binge Drinking and Addiction

Binge drinking is common in the United States. According to the CDC, one in six adults binge drinks approximately four times each month. Both high school and college students consume large amounts of alcohol in a short about of time as well. According to the CDC, adults between the ages of eighteen and thirty-five binge drink most frequently.

Binge drinking poses serious health risks. The CDC notes that approximately 88,000 people die from large amounts of alcohol consumption each year. In addition, binge drinking increases the drinkers' risk for "a number of health and social problems, including unintentional injuries, interpersonal violence, suicide, alcohol poisoning, high blood pressure, heart disease and stroke, cancer, liver disease, and severe alcohol use disorder," says the CDC.[38]

> **Binge drinking increases "a number of health and social problems, including unintentional injuries, interpersonal violence, suicide, alcohol poisoning, high blood pressure, heart disease and stroke, cancer, liver disease, and severe alcohol use disorder."[38]**
>
> —Centers for Disease Control and Prevention

Colleges across the nation are not doing much to curb binge drinking. This is despite the large number of students that are sexually assaulted each year in alcohol-related situations. However, a recent focus on campus sexual assault has swept through the nation. Some prevention advocates are hopeful that this will cause colleges to pay more attention to binge drinking.

Binge drinking can harm people's organs. One organ that can be severely impacted is the liver.

Other advocates are hoping the financial cost of binge drinking will motivate colleges to make changes. Jonathan Gibralter, the president of Frostburg State University in Maryland, found that four years of alcohol abuse totaled $1 million in lost tuition and staff time. He noted that if people recognize how much the issue costs, people will work harder to stop binge drinking.

Living with a Parent Who Struggles with Addiction

Addiction impacts the person struggling with it, but he or she is not the only one affected. Experts have found that everyone in a family with an addicted person is affected in some way by the addiction. For instance, addiction impacts the family's finances and peoples' physical health and mental well-being. This impact is overwhelmingly negative.

Often, children don't understand why a parent can't stop using harmful substances. Their parent's drug or alcohol use can lead to a lot of resentment.

Children especially suffer when they live with a parent who has an addiction. The effects of living with an addicted parent are present long after childhood has ended. Living with an addicted parent can cause low self-esteem, a poor self-image, guilt, loneliness, and anxiety. It also can lead to feelings of helplessness, fear of abandonment, and even chronic depression.

The number of people who have lived with an addicted parent is staggering. According to the National Association for Children of Alcoholics, a charity that aims to end the impact of drug and alcohol use on families, "One in four youth under the age of 18 lives in a family where a person abuses alcohol or suffers from alcoholism. Countless others are affected by a family member's use of drugs."[39] What's more, children of people with alcohol use disorder are four times more likely to have alcohol use disorder than individuals who did not have an addicted parent.

For children and teens of addicted parents, their home life is often unstable, disorganized, and chaotic. They live with the uncertainty of not knowing whether their parent is going to be sober. They are also often unsupervised and left to fend for themselves. In addition, the financial consequences of addiction can cause the children and teens in the household to be underfed and undereducated. When children grow up with one or more people who struggle with addiction, they often miss out on many of the things their peers experience and live in a constant state of uncertainty. There is often no stability. "Alcohol misuse and substance use are exceedingly common in this country, and parents' or caregivers' substance use may affect their ability to consistently prioritize their children's basic physical and emotional needs and provide a safe, nurturing environment," explains Vincent C. Smith, who is an assistant professor at Harvard Medical School.[40]

What's more, children may be exposed to illegal activities, such as the purchase of illegal drugs. They may even be asked to lie to police, children's services, and school officials about what their parents are doing. They may also watch their parent deal with unemployment, legal issues,

"Alcohol misuse and substance use are exceedingly common in this country, and parents' or caregivers' substance use may affect their ability to consistently prioritize their children's basic physical and emotional needs and provide a safe, nurturing environment."[40]

—Vincent C. Smith, assistant professor at Harvard Medical School mental illness, and divorce—all of which can place a heavy burden on the children.

Addiction and Family Roles

Experts who study addiction and family life have noticed that many family members assume specific roles within the family when someone is coping with addiction. These roles are often a subconscious way of attempting to help the family function better.

One role is the enabler. This role is usually filled by a parent who does not struggle with addiction. It could also be filled by an older child, especially in single-parent families. Someone who enables often takes care of everything that the person struggling with addiction is unable to do. This might include paying the bills, taking care of

If parents are struggling with addiction, an older child will sometimes take over the role of parent for younger siblings. This can put a lot of stress on the older child.

the chores, preparing all the meals, and making sure children go to school. An enabler might also make excuses or justify the addicted person's actions, especially in social situations or with employers.

Another role is known as the hero. Typically, the oldest child in the family will take on this role, which involves overachieving, acting serious, and appearing confident. According to Mary Egan, who is an outreach director at Rosecrance, a treatment center, children take on these types of roles "to cope with an unnatural situation."[41] Many times, heroes will assume responsibilities that are too mature for their age. This includes taking on some parenting responsibilities. What's more, the hero is usually a perfectionist. But this perfectionism becomes hard to keep up as the addicted person's disease progresses.

In an unstable home caused by addiction, it is not uncommon to find a person who uses humor to cope. This role is known as the mascot. The mascot is usually aware that his or her behavior brings feelings of relief to the people around him or her. As a result, he or she will continue this behavior because it brings a level of comfort to the family.

The scapegoat is a child who frequently misbehaves and is defiant. Typically, the scapegoat will act out both at home and in school. As the scapegoat gets older, he or she may experience issues with the law. The misbehavior of the scapegoat is reflective of the chaos at home.

The lost child is a family member who is usually isolated and has issues developing relationships. The lost child is often forgotten and lonely. At home, the lost child might find ways to distract herself or mentally distance herself from the situation. She often removes herself from the family dynamic and spends time away from the home.

The person with the addiction is the last role in the family structure. Some people who are struggling with addiction feel guilt, shame, and sadness for the pain they have created at home. However, some addicted people don't view their substance abuse

A CLOSER LOOK AT CODEPENDENCY

The concept of codependency became popular in the 1980s. Since then, the use of the word has declined somewhat, but it is still an important concept to understand when dealing with addiction. Codependency refers to a person who is overly involved with a person who is struggling with addiction.

For instance, a codependent individual often puts the needs of the addicted person ahead of his own, even when doing so hurts his health or well-being. A codependent person will often defend or make excuses for the person who is struggling with addiction. He also might try to fix the person or control his or her substance abuse. He may even try to remain in the addicted person's favor by attempting to meet his or her every need and not disagree or get angry with him or her.

Until a codependent person learns how to address his own issues, he is not helping the person who is struggling with addiction. Instead, a codependent person needs to learn how to set healthy boundaries and not enable the addicted person. The best way to deal with addiction is to hold the person struggling with addiction accountable for her choices, set clear boundaries, and to allow her to experience the consequences of her choices.

as an issue. This can lead to much resentment and anger from other family members.

Addiction and Its Impact on Society

Addiction also has a large impact on society. Not only do people have to deal with the fact that addiction is everywhere, but it is a costly problem to address. Estimates on the total overall costs of addressing addiction top $600 billion annually in the United States, according to NCADD.

Law enforcement plays a vital role in the war on drugs. One of its responsibilities is catching drug dealers.

This figure not only represents health care–related costs but also includes crime-related costs, as well as lost productivity. Of the $600 billion, approximately $235 billion is spent on alcohol alone. Meanwhile, the remaining $365 billion is split between costs for dealing with tobacco issues and illicit drugs. "As staggering as these numbers are, they do not fully describe the breadth of destructive public health and safety implications of drug abuse and addiction, such as family disintegration, loss of employment, failure in school, domestic violence, and child abuse," warns NCADD.[42] But the good news is that while addiction is a horrible disease with severe consequences, it is both treatable and preventable.

Chapter 4

HOW CAN PEOPLE COPE WITH ADDICTION?

Growing up in the suburbs of Philadelphia, Pennsylvania, Kelly Fitzgerald wanted desperately to fit in with the kids she perceived as cool. She even took a class in middle school on how to make friends. But she felt like nothing worked until she started drinking.

Fitzgerald was fifteen years old when she had her first drink. She raided her parents' liquor cabinet with a friend, drank gin, and eventually threw up in the sink. Despite getting sick, she liked the way the alcohol made her feel. She felt relaxed and funny. "I became the popular girl I had always wanted to be," she says. "I never thought it could escalate or that I would wake up one day and ask: 'Who am I? What am I doing? How did it get to this point?'"[43]

Fitzgerald's drinking got progressively worse as the years went on. She didn't realize she needed to stop drinking or that she might have an addiction. Even when she started having blackouts and missing work, she thought it was normal. It wasn't until her boyfriend ended things with her that she realized she had a problem and needed to quit. "I said enough. I told myself I was done drinking and using. I decided to try something new: stopping all together," Fitzgerald said.[44]

She admitted the first few days after she quit were some of the hardest days of her life. She felt very alone and was ashamed of herself. She also had to deal with symptoms of alcohol withdrawal. Fitzgerald could not stop sweating, her stomach hurt, and she could not sleep. Getting through those first few days was not easy, but as her body adjusted, her recovery got easier. "I always like to say 'you're not alone,'" Fitzgerald says. "Everyone feels like they're the only person with this problem, or the only person feeling this way."[45]

> "I said enough. I told myself I was done drinking and using. I decided to try something new: stopping all together."[44]
>
> —Kelly Fitzgerald, recovering from alcohol addiction

Now that she's sober, Fitzgerald says life is much more enjoyable. "I think alcohol plays tricks on you. It makes you think: 'this is the best party ever!'" Fitzgerald says. "Drugs and alcohol helped me never feel satisfied. I was always looking for more, more, more. Now I am satisfied with waking up and seeing a beautiful sunrise and being alive. That's enough."[46]

Making a decision to quit, like Fitzgerald did, is the first step in addiction recovery. For many people struggling with addiction this is the hardest step. But once they recognize that they have a problem and make a choice to change, they are well on their way to addressing their addiction.

In the beginning, when a person first decides to quit, she may feel uncertain about whether or not she is ready to change, or if it is even possible. These feelings and concerns are normal. The key is not to let the uncertainty derail the fight for freedom from drugs or alcohol. It is never easy, but it can be done. There is also a variety of programs that aim to prevent teen drug use before addiction sets in.

Prevention Strategies

According to NIDA, drug prevention for teens is important, since early drug abuse can increase a teen's chance of developing an addiction. Transition periods in a teen's life are especially risky, as teens can turn to substances to cope. One example of a transition period is changing schools. In addition, as children grow up they are usually exposed to more substances and partake in more risk-seeking behavior.

There is a variety of research-based programs that aim at preventing young adults from falling into substance abuse. According to NIDA, "Studies have shown that research-based programs . . . can significantly reduce early use of tobacco, alcohol, and illicit drugs."[47] NIDA also notes that prevention programs should educate students on various types of drug abuse, discuss specific drug problems within the community, and target at-risk students.

Identifying at-risk children can be done with the Adverse Childhood Experiences (ACEs) model. SAMHSA explains that ACEs are traumatic or stressful events that children have gone through. These events can include sexual or physical abuse, domestic violence, emotional abuse, substance abuse at home, parent divorce, or incarceration of someone the child lived with. According to SAMHSA, the more ACEs a child has, the more at risk she is for substance abuse. High ACE scores also play a role in the age a person begins using alcohol. Professionals can spot at risk children and intervene to help prevent these issues.

Drug prevention programs can be found in schools. According to NIDA, effective school-based programs focus on strengthening relationships between peers, developing drug-refusal techniques, and enhance coping skills and self-control. One school-based prevention program was founded in 1983 and is known as the Drug Abuse Resistance Education (D.A.R.E.) program. D.A.R.E. began as

Former First Lady Nancy Reagan, third from right, supported drug prevention programs such as D.A.R.E. However, D.A.R.E. ultimately proved to be ineffective.

a collaboration between public schools in Los Angeles, California, and the city's police department. The program soon spread across the nation. Police officers went into classrooms to discuss drugs with students and encourage them to resist trying drugs. However, research in the early 1990s showed that the program wasn't decreasing drug use among teens.

In 2009, the D.A.R.E. organization changed its technique and began the keepin' it REAL program. REAL is an acronym for Refuse, Explain, Avoid, and Leave. Instead of lecturing students about drugs, keepin' it REAL uses interactive activities that show students how to make smart choices. The program is used in elementary and middle schools around the country and has shown to be more effective than the D.A.R.E. program.

Another school-based program is called Project ALERT. This prevention program targets seventh and eighth graders and focuses on preventing teen use of tobacco, marijuana, alcohol, and inhalants. According to SAMHSA, Project ALERT has proven effective in its goal. Other drug prevention programs recommended by NIDA include Caring School Community Program, which strengthens children's ties to the community while reducing drug use, and the Life Skills Training Program, which targets middle school students and teaches them drug resistance techniques.

Lifestyle Changes

When substance abuse prevention doesn't work and people become addicted to drugs, a commitment to sobriety requires people to make some changes in their lives. At the top of the list is changing the way they deal with stress. Many people who struggle with addiction often turn to alcohol and drugs to cope with difficult emotions. But this is an unhealthy coping mechanism. If an addicted person is committed to recovery, she will need to find healthy ways of coping with life's challenges.

Another change that people struggling with addiction will need to make is determining who they allow in their lives. If all of their friends are using drugs or abusing alcohol, their recovery will impact those relationships. People coping with addiction cannot continue to spend time with people who no longer have the same goals that they do. This change is usually difficult, but it is necessary to achieve sobriety.

In addition, people recovering from addiction need to think about how they are going to spend their free time. This may be hard at first. After all, addiction is a huge time thief. It robbed the person struggling with addiction of many hours, days, and perhaps years. Most people who have an addiction spend a large amount of time and resources feeding their addiction. But in order to cope with addiction,

Changing an addicted person's environment can be beneficial to her recovery. It can help reduce the chance of triggers that will make her think about drugs.

they will need to find new, healthier ways to spend their time. This might mean taking up a new hobby, exercising, reading, journaling, or a combination of these things. The key is that they do not allow themselves to have too much time where the temptation to use drugs or alcohol will creep back in.

People preparing to quit also will need to address how they view themselves. It is not uncommon for people with addictions to have low self-esteem. They also may feel a lot of guilt and shame over the things they have done. While these feelings are normal for someone who struggles with addiction, they are not healthy and should be addressed. People recovering from addiction need to realize that they still have value and worth. Addiction is a disease, and they can learn to manage it. Once they realize that, they can learn to be a lot more compassionate toward themselves.

What Addiction Recovery Entails

Once a person makes a commitment to address addiction, it helps to have a clear understanding of what treatment entails. There are many different ways to cope with addiction, and there is no one-size-fits-all approach when it comes to treatment. The best programs are the ones that are tailored to meet each person's specific needs.

Detoxification is an important step to recovery. The person struggling with addiction needs to purge his body of the drugs or alcohol and may need assistance managing any withdrawal symptoms. Allowing the body to get used to living without a substance that it has become dependent on is not an easy task, but it is doable.

People recovering from addiction will also need counseling to address any underlying issues that may have contributed to the addiction. Working with a counselor allows them to learn how to modify their behavior and discover the root causes of their drug or alcohol use. The goal with counseling is to provide healthier ways to cope with negative situations as well as to help repair relationships that were damaged by addiction. Counseling can take place in individual, group, or family settings.

NIDA notes that sometimes people struggling with addiction may need prescriptions to help them manage and deal with withdrawal symptoms. They may also be prescribed medication to help prevent relapse. And if they have a coexisting condition such as depression, they will need to be treated for that issue as well. Each issue will need to be addressed separately. Sometimes people make the mistake of thinking that giving up drugs or alcohol will make the mental health issues go away. But that is usually not the case. For instance, the symptoms of depression may be eased when the person is no longer using drugs or alcohol, but the depression will still need to be addressed.

It is not uncommon for someone with an addiction to relapse. The best way to prevent relapse is for the addicted person to continue getting support for his addiction. This might include attending meetings with support groups and receiving counseling. "Self-help groups . . . play a vital role in substance abuse treatment in the United States, and research has shown that active involvement in support groups significantly improves the likelihood of remaining clean and sober," NCADD says.[48]

In support groups, the members share a common problem, such as an addiction to drugs or alcohol. Support groups can be in a variety of different forms. For instance, two people meeting to share their coping strategies can be considered a support group, as can a small group of people gathering to meet. The key is that members of the group hold one another accountable and provide a safe place to talk about the challenges of recovery.

> **"Self-help groups . . . play a vital role in substance abuse treatment in the United States, and research has shown that active involvement in support groups significantly improves the likelihood of remaining clean and sober."[48]**
>
> —National Council on Alcoholism and Drug Dependence

Types of Treatment Programs

When it comes to dealing with teen addiction, the American Society of Addiction Medicine has developed a set of guidelines for determining the length of treatment that teens need. To make treatment recommendations, doctors and counselors typically review several areas of the teen's life.

The first thing they look at is how significant the drug use is, as well as the potential for withdrawal. Then they screen the teen for the presence of other medical conditions as well as any emotional or behavioral issues. They also consider a teen's readiness to change, the risk of relapse, and what type of recovery environment she has. Overall, the goal is to make sure the treatment is long enough and strong enough to be effective.

There are several types of treatment programs for young people recovering from addiction. These include outpatient treatment, partial hospitalization, and inpatient treatment. Inpatient treatment means the person must be admitted to the hospital or rehab facility for treatment, while outpatient treatment allows the person to return home after treatment. Most of the time, addiction recovery for teens is offered in outpatient settings. These situations can be highly effective as long as the health professionals are well trained. Typically, this option is recommended for teens whose addictions are not severe. Also, the teens benefitting from outpatient treatment usually do not have additional mental health issues and have a supportive home environment. Most outpatient programs offer at least two sessions per week for about three hours each. But more intensive programs may meet more frequently or for longer periods of time.

Some teens benefit from partial hospitalization. In this situation, teens participate in day treatment while still living at home. They attend treatment for four to six hours per day, five days a week, but return home after each session. During outpatient treatment and partial hospitalization programs, people trust that the teen will not continue using drugs or alcohol while not in treatment.

Finally, inpatient treatment provides a high level of care and is generally needed for teens with severe addictions who also might have mental health issues or other medical needs. In inpatient programs, patients live in a twenty-four-hour structured environment. Typically, the teens in these programs have complex mental health issues or family problems that interfere with their ability to recover from addiction. In this setting, teens receive treatment that focuses

WHY IS QUITTING SO HARD?

Almost every person struggling with addiction believes that she can stop using drugs or alcohol on her own, and many people try to stop without treatment. According to NIDA, in 2011 more than 20 million people older than age twelve needed treatment for an alcohol or drug problem. However, only 2.3 million people got treatment at a facility.

Although some people might be successful in quitting without help, many people fail to stay sober for long. Part of this has to do with the lack of support they would otherwise get from being in a treatment program. The fact that addiction is a chronic brain disease that cannot be cured also plays a part. Research has shown that using drugs or alcohol for a long period of time changes the brain, and these changes exist long after a person stops using drugs or alcohol. This is especially true because addiction alters a person's ability control impulses related to drugs or alcohol. For this reason, the person struggles with constantly wanting to use drugs and alcohol. These changes to the brain's wiring can be seen in brain imaging studies of people who suffer from addiction. The brain of someone with an addiction has been forever altered. As a result, she can learn to cope with her addiction, but she will have to manage the consequences of addiction for their rest of her life.

on building personal and social responsibility while developing new coping skills. Sometimes the programs require family members to participate in the recovery process. What this usually means is that they need to participate in family counseling sessions. Meanwhile, there are some people who pick less traditional treatment options such as prayer groups, religious practices, and quitting without medical involvement.

Coping with a Friend or Family Member's Addiction

According to SAMHSA, when a person realizes that someone she cares about is addicted to drugs or alcohol, it can feel overwhelming. She may not know what to do or how to help, or she may think she can fix the addicted person's situation. Although she cannot control another person's addiction or make that person quit, she can be supportive. "Often these family members and friends struggle to provide support while simultaneously coping with feelings of betrayal, anger and fear. It can be a confusing time for family members and friends," explains Elizabeth Donnellan, a professor at Kaplan University in Minnesota.[49]

To help cope with a loved one's addiction, Donnellan suggests beginning by understanding the addiction process. This information helps a person recognize why achieving sobriety can be such a struggle. She also suggests family counseling as a way of coping. "Family members often have complicated emotions related to the loved one's addiction and former actions," she says. "When people are addicted to drugs or alcohol, their focus is on the addiction and not on the well-being of family and friends. This can leave family members with anger towards the loved one particularly if he or she lied or stole to accommodate the addiction."[50]

Donnellan also suggests setting boundaries so that everyone in the family knows what is acceptable and what is unacceptable. Boundaries are especially important in the beginning stages of recovery and help support a healthy family environment. "Addiction treatment takes time to work, and for some people, a lot of time," Donnellan says. "Patience, love, direct communication and acceptance of the difficulty of recovery are the best ways to support those you care about most."[51]

How Effective Is Addiction Treatment?

The goal of addiction recovery is not only stopping the substance abuse but also addressing any underlying issues such as depression, stress management, grief, and loneliness so that the person with the addiction can become a productive part of his or her family and community. According to NIDA, most people in treatment stop abusing substances, reduce their criminal activities, and improve their psychological functioning.

Overall, a person's treatment outcome depends on how severe his problems are, combined with the type of treatment and other services he receives. But just like any other chronic disease, addiction can be managed with success. Appropriate treatment allows people to deal effectively with addiction's powerful effects on the brain and to regain control of their lives.

"When people are addicted to drugs or alcohol, their focus is on the addiction and not on the well-being of family and friends. This can leave family members with anger towards the loved one particularly if he or she lied or stole to accommodate the addiction."[50]

—Elizabeth Donnellan, professor at Kaplan University

Speaking to a drug counselor can be helpful for a teen with an addiction. Drug counselors are trained to provide support and encourage recovery.

How to Handle Relapses

Since addiction is a chronic disease, the likelihood that the person struggling with addiction will relapse is high. The possibility for relapse is much like any other chronic disease. Some people interpret a relapse to mean that the treatment has failed, but this is not the case. A relapse is a signal that treatment needs to be reinstated or adjusted. Or it might mean that the person needs an alternative treatment. Successful treatment for addiction requires continued evaluation and modification, just like for any other disease.

Relapses are typically caused by triggers. Triggers are things in a person's life that put the person at risk of falling into old patterns of substance abuse. Some examples might include negative emotions such as anger, sadness, and stress. Dr. Rajita Sinha at Yale University School of Medicine examined the relationship between stress and alcohol abuse: "It has long been known that stress increases the risk of alcohol relapse. . . . Chronic alcohol use can result in neuroadaptive changes in stress and reward pathways. Such changes may alter an alcohol-dependent person's response to stress . . . which in turn may increase the risk of relapse."[52]

Conflict with others as well as social pressures can also be triggers for drug or alcohol abuse. Withdrawal symptoms, physical pain, and cravings also can cause a person to relapse. Sometimes, people struggling with addiction will want to test their personal control. They tell themselves that they can have just one drink or just one pill. But for someone with an addiction, these attempts are rarely successful.

While relapses can be disappointing, they are not a reason to give up on recovery. They are an opportunity for the person struggling with addiction to learn from her mistakes, identify additional triggers, and correct her treatment plan. If a relapse does occur, the person recovering from addiction should reach out for help. This may mean meeting with a doctor, talking to a counselor, or calling a treatment facility.

A Life Free of Addiction

When recovering from an addiction, it's important for an individual to build a life that will not only keep him free from substance abuse, but will also give his life meaning and purpose. The best way to do that is for him to find activities and interests that he is passionate about. He should pick things that he enjoys and that make him feel needed. Once the recovering person's life is filled with rewarding activities and interests, the addiction will lose its appeal.

SAMHSA notes that volunteering in the community could be one way to accomplish this. Giving back to others in a meaningful way can be a rewarding experience for many people. Individuals can look for opportunities to serve others through nearby faith communities or local schools. People can also join a local club or a neighborhood group that supports the community in some way. In a 2009 article published in *Alcoholism Treatment Quarterly*, the article's researchers say, "Helping others provides a therapeutic benefit to the helper. The mental health benefits of helping others have been well documented: mood improves, depression and anxiety decrease, self-esteem increases, and purpose of life is enhanced."[53]

Another option for people in recovery is to consider adopting a pet if they have the resources and time to care for it properly. Cats and dogs have a way of making people feel loved and needed. Research has shown that petting a dog or cat can reduce stress levels in people. Although they are an added responsibility, having an animal that depends on a person for food and exercise can give an addicted person's life meaning.

> **"Exercise is increasingly becoming a component of many treatment programs and has proven effective."[54]**
>
> —National Institute on Drug Abuse

People recovering from addiction also need to stay healthy. Exercising regularly and eating right does wonders for the body. Plus, exercise is a great stress reliever and can help people manage negative feelings or emotions. NIDA notes that "exercise is increasingly becoming a component of many treatment programs and has proven effective."[54]

People in recovery should also be sure to get plenty of sleep so that they keep their brains fresh and alert. When people have sleep deficits they tend to make poor decisions. It's important for people to do everything they can to support their recovery.

Looking for opportunities to relax and to appreciate the little things in life also helps with addiction recovery. One example of this is taking time to enjoy nature. Many people think taking a walk through a park or a hike in the woods is relaxing. The views are sometimes breathtaking and the fresh air can be invigorating. Another activity to help recovery could be taking advantage of a community's arts programs.

According to SAMHSA, another way to fill the time that was once filled with addiction is to take up a hobby. Whether it is something the person in recovery once enjoyed or something completely new, challenging herself in some way can have all types of rewards. Some examples might be learning to play the guitar, trying a new sport, or learning a foreign language. The idea is to find an activity that is enjoyable and helps the person fill the space in her life that used to be consumed by drugs or alcohol.

People in recovery should set realistic goals for themselves. Having something to work toward as well as something to look forward to can be powerful antidotes to addiction. One example of a goal could be to create a list of things a person would like to do or see, and then to make a plan for how those things might happen. It doesn't matter what his goals are, as long as they are attainable and have meaning to him. The key is to keep the goals realistic, because if he does not reach them, then he might experience a sense of failure. This could be a trigger for him.

It's important for people in recovery to be patient with themselves. Overcoming addiction is not an easy task, but with hard work and perseverance an addicted person can do it. As Fitzgerald realized when she stopped drinking: "There is a grieving period [during addiction recovery]. It's like a breakup. You have to give yourself time to get over it."[55]

RECOGNIZING SIGNS OF TROUBLE

Signs of Addiction

- Is frequently late or absent from school or work
- Experiences difficulty in relationships with other people
- Has a significant change in weight, such as becoming very thin or gaining a great deal of weight
- Has mood swings, gets angry easily, or displays drastic changes in personality
- Stops spending time with family and friends
- Starts hanging out with a new group of friends
- Seems nervous or jumpy
- Disappears for long periods of time with no explanation
- Steals money, prescriptions, and valuables

Symptoms of Addiction

- Needing to use the drug on a regular basis
- Experiencing strong urges to use the drug
- Developing a tolerance to the drug
- Focusing a large amount of time on finding and getting the drug
- Spending money to obtain the drug when the person cannot afford to do so
- Neglecting responsibilities at work or at home
- Using the drug even when it's causing issues, such as social, physical, or psychological problems
- Being unable to stop using the drug

ORGANIZATIONS TO CONTACT

Al-Anon Family Groups

al-anon.org

Al-Anon is a support group for friends and families of people who abuse alcohol.

American Association for the Treatment of Opioid Dependence

www.aatod.org

The American Association for the Treatment of Opioid Dependence works with state and federal governments to explore policies for opioid treatment.

Center on Addiction

www.centeronaddiction.org

Center on Addiction is a nonprofit organization that aims to end the addiction crisis in the United States.

Centers for Disease Control and Prevention

www.cdc.gov

The Centers for Disease Control and Prevention aims to protect people from health threats.

National Council on Alcoholism and Drug Dependence (NCADD)

www.ncadd.org

NCADD is a health organization that works to help people addicted to drugs and alcohol. NCADD offers school-based education programs, referral services, and treatment programs.

SOURCE NOTES

Introduction: What Does Addiction Look Like?

1. Quoted in Tracey Helton Mitchell, "Heroin: Stories of Addiction," *Healthline*, July 29, 2014. healthline.com.

2. Quoted in Mitchell, "Heroin: Stories of Addiction."

3. Quoted in "Understanding Drug Use and Addiction," *National Institute on Drug Abuse*, August 2016. drugabuse.gov.

4. Quoted in Mitchell, "Heroin: Stories of Addiction."

5. Quoted in "Principles of Drug Addiction Treatment: A Research-Based Guide (Third Edition)," *National Institute on Drug Abuse*, January 2018. drugabuse.gov.

Chapter 1: What Is Addiction?

6. Quoted in "Demi Lovato: Simply Complicated—Official Documentary," *YouTube*, October 17, 2017. youtube.com.

7. Quoted in "Demi Lovato: Simply Complicated—Official Documentary."

8. Quoted in "Demi Lovato: Simply Complicated—Official Documentary."

9. Quoted in "Demi Lovato: Simply Complicated—Official Documentary."

10. Quoted in Megan Armstrong, "The 10 Most Honest Confessions from Demi Lovato's 'Simply Complicated' YouTube Documentary," *Billboard*, October 18, 2017. billboard.com.

11. Quoted in Armstrong, "The 10 Most Honest Confessions from Demi Lovato's 'Simply Complicated' YouTube Documentary."

12. Quoted in Armstrong, "The 10 Most Honest Confessions from Demi Lovato's 'Simply Complicated' YouTube Documentary."

13. Quoted in Seyyed Salman Alavi, et al, "Behavioral Addiction Versus Substance Addiction: Correspondence of Psychiatric and Psychological Views," *International Journal of Preventive Medicine,* April 2012. ncbi.nlm.nih.gov.

14. Quoted in Michael Botticelli, "Addiction Is a Disease. We Should Treat It Like One," *TED*, n.d. ted.com.

15. Quoted in "Top 8 Reasons Why Teens Try Alcohol and Drugs." *Partnership for Drug-Free Kids*, February 13, 2017. drugfree.org.

16. Quoted in "Top 8 Reasons Why Teens Try Alcohol and Drugs."

Chapter 2: What Causes Addiction?

17. Quoted in "Families and Drug Use: 'I Feel So Helpless Against His Addiction,'" *National Institute on Drug Abuse*, n.d. easyread.drugabuse.gov.

18. Quoted in "Families and Drug Use: 'I Feel So Helpless Against His Addiction.'"

19. Quoted in "Families and Drug Use: 'I Feel So Helpless Against His Addiction.'"

20. Quoted in "Principles of Adolescent Substance Use Disorder Treatment: A Research-Based Guide," *National Institute on Drug Abuse*, January 2014. drugabuse.gov.

21. Quoted in "Understanding Addiction," *NCADD*, July 25, 2015. ncadd.org.

22. Quoted in "Principles of Adolescent Substance Use Disorder Treatment: A Research-Based Guide."

23. Quoted in "Principles of Adolescent Substance Use Disorder Treatment: A Research-Based Guide."

24. Quoted in "Understanding Addiction."

25. Quoted in "Principles of Drug Addiction Treatment: A Research-Based Guide (Third Edition)," *National Institute on Drug Abuse*, January 2018. drugabuse.gov.

26. Quoted in Mike Adams, "Science Says There's No Such Thing as an 'Addictive Personality,'" *High Times*, November 10, 2017. hightimes.com.

27. Quoted in "Teen Substance Use," *Center on Addiction*, n.d. centeronaddiction.org.

28. Quoted in "Genes and Addiction," *Genetic Science Learning Center*, n.d. learn.genetics.utah.edu.

Chapter 3: What Are the Effects of Addiction?

29. Quoted in Jeremy Peppas, "Drug Take Back Day Is Saturday," *Jacksonville Patriot*, April 25, 2017. pulaskinews.net.

30. Quoted in Thomas J. Gould, "Addiction and Cognition," *NCBI*, December 2010. ncbi.nlm.nih.gov.

31. Quoted in German Lopez, "The Opioid Epidemic Explained," *Vox*, December 21, 2017. vox.com.

32. Quoted in "Health Consequences of Drug Misuse," *National Institute on Drug Abuse*, March 2017. drugabuse.gov.

33. Quoted in Tim Newman, "Cannabis and Schizophrenia: New Evidence Unveiled," *Medical News Today*, April 28, 2017. medicalnewstoday.com.

34. Quoted in "Smoking & Tobacco Use," *CDC*, n.d. cdc.gov.

35. Quoted in "MDMA (Ecstasy/Molly)," *National Institute on Drug Abuse*, October 2016. drugabuse.gov.

36. Quoted in Richard G. Soper, "Intimate Partner Violence and Co-Occurring Substance Abuse/Addiction," *ASAM*, October 6, 2014. asam.org.

37. Quoted in "Underage and College Drinking," *NCADD*, June 27, 2015. ncadd.org.

38. Quoted in Jamie Ducharme, "Binge Drinkers Have About 7 Drinks at a Time, CDC Says," *Time*, March 16, 2018. time.com.

39. Quoted in "It's Not Your Fault!" *SAMHSA*, n.d. store.samhsa.gov.

40. Quoted in Christopher Bergland, "Harvard Study Pegs How Parental Substance Abuse Impacts Kids," *Psychology Today*, July 18, 2016. psychologytoday.com.

41. Quoted in "Addiction and the Family: What Are the Roles That Emerge?" *Chicago Tribune*, August 11, 2015. chicagotribune.com.

42. Quoted in "Understanding Addiction," *NCADD*, July 25, 2015. ncadd.org.

Chapter 4: How Can People Cope with Addiction?

43. Quoted in "Recovery Stories: Kelly Fitzgerald," *Drug Rehab*, n.d. drugrehab.com.

44. Quoted in "Recovery Stories: Kelly Fitzgerald."

45. Quoted in "Recovery Stories: Kelly Fitzgerald."

46. Quoted in "Recovery Stories: Kelly Fitzgerald."

47. Quoted in "Drugs, Brains, and Behavior: The Science of Addiction," *National Institute on Drug Abuse*, July 2014. drugabuse.gov.

48. Quoted in "Self-Help/Recovery Support Groups," *NCADD*, April 2, 2018. ncadd.org.

49. Quoted in Elizabeth Donnellan, "4 Tools to Help the Families of People Fighting Addiction (Op-Ed)," *LiveScience*, September 11, 2015. livescience.com.

50. Quoted in Elizabeth Donnellan, "4 Tools to Help the Families of People Fighting Addiction (Op-Ed)."

51. Quoted in Elizabeth Donnellan, "4 Tools to Help the Families of People Fighting Addiction (Op-Ed)."

52. Quoted in Rajita Sinha, "How Does Stress Lead to Risk of Alcohol Relapse?" *National Institute on Alcohol Abuse and Alcoholism*, n.d. pubs.niaaa.nih.gov.

53. Quoted in Maria E. Pagano, et al, "Helping Others and Long-Term Sobriety: Who Should I Help to Stay Sober?" *NCBI*, January 2009. ncbi.nlm.nih.gov.

54. Quoted in "Principles of Drug Addiction Treatment: A Research-Based Guide (Third Edition)," *National Institute on Drug Abuse*, January 2018. drugabuse.gov.

55. Quoted in "Recovery Stories: Kelly Fitzgerald."

FOR FURTHER RESEARCH

BOOKS

Marylou Ambrose, *Investigate Alcohol*. Berkeley Heights, NJ: Enslow, 2015.

Tracy Brown Hamilton, *I Am Addicted to Drugs: Now What?* New York: Rosen, 2017.

Susan Henneberg, *Defeating Addiction and Alcoholism*. New York: Rosen, 2016.

Elizabeth Herschbach, *Teens and Mental Health*. San Diego: ReferencePoint Press, 2019.

Barbara Gottfried Hollander, *Addiction*. New York: Rosen, 2012.

INTERNET SOURCES

MIH MedlinePlus, *The Science of Addiction: Drugs, Brains, and Behavior*, Spring 2007. medlineplus.gov.

National Institute on Drug Abuse, *Understanding Drug Use and Addiction*, August 2016. www.drugabuse.gov.

WEBSITES

Alcoholics Anonymous

www.aa.org

Alcoholics Anonymous is a twelve-step recovery program that helps people struggling with alcohol use disorder.

American Society of Addiction Medicine

www.asam.org

The American Society of Addiction Medicine offers a nationwide directory of addiction medicine professionals.

National Alliance on Mental Illness

www.nami.org

This organization helps families dealing with a variety of mental disorders.

National Suicide Prevention Lifeline

suicidepreventionlifeline.org

The National Suicide Prevention Lifeline offers suicide prevention services and can help in a lot of other areas too, including drug and alcohol abuse. They also can connect individuals with a nearby professional.

Substance Abuse and Mental Health Services Administration

www.findtreatment.samhsa.gov

This organization shows the location of inpatient, outpatient, and hospital inpatient treatment programs for drug addiction and alcoholism throughout the country.

INDEX

IMAGE CREDITS

ABOUT THE AUTHOR

Sherri Mabry Gordon is a bullying prevention advocate and the author of nearly twenty nonfiction books. Many of her books deal with issues teens face today, including bullying, abuse, public shaming, online safety, and more. Gordon has given multiple presentations to schools, churches, and the YMCA on bullying prevention, dating abuse, and online safety. She also serves on the School Counselor Advisory Board for two schools. Gordon resides in Columbus, Ohio, with her husband, two children, and dog Abbey.